Lessons in Breathing Underwater

Sundress Publications • Knoxville, TN

Editor: Jeremy Michael Reed
Editorial Assistant: Anna Black
Editorial Interns: Maria Esquinca and Erica Hoffmeister

Colophon: This book is set in Goudy Old Style.

Cover Image: Kristen Ton

Cover Design: Kristen Ton

Book Design: Erin Elizabeth Smith

Lessons in Breathing Underwater
H.K. Hummel

Acknowledgements

I am grateful to the Arkansas Arts Council for supporting this work, as well as the editors of the journals and anthologies where many of these poems first appeared, sometimes in slightly different forms:

100 Word Story: "Life by Bicycle"
Booth: "Yesterday's Bestiary for Tomorrow," and "If You and I Said
   Fuck It, and Bought the Ranch in Montana"
Coldnoon: International Journal of Travel Writing: "The Compass Rose
   Spins like a Ouija Board Planchette"
The Examined Life Journal: "Scintigraphy"
Forgotten Women (Grayson Books): "Elizabeth Eckford's Walk Toward
   Central High School"
Fourth River: "Urban Self-Portrait"
Heron Tree: "That August"
Hudson Review: "Conception"
Iron Horse Review: "Jeanne Baret, After Tahiti"
J Journal: New Writing on Justice: "After Bikini Atoll"
Meridian: "Vigil," and "To Begin"
Requited: "Magritte's *Golconda* as Treatise on Post-traumatic Stress
   Disorder I and II," and "This Body Fixed in Place"
Short-Form Creative Writing: A Writer's Guide and Anthology: "If You
   Hand Me the Right Map," "Tonight, At the Santee Drive-In
   Movie Theatre," "Talk to Me: A Wunderkammer," and
   "Terra Incognita"
Stone House: A Literary Anthology: "At Daybreak"
Talking Writing: "All We Don't Know"

"Lullaby in Blue" first appeared in *Flock Lit*'s album, *This Is For You: Twelve Lullabies*.

Table of Contents

IV. BREATHE AGAIN

Night has turned to day, lord mama
oh, night has turned to day.
—The Fantastic Negrito

Everything Goes Deeper Than You Expect

You find yourself on life support,
and you have no recollection
of how you got here.

Strangers have fallen in love with you,
fought for you, while you slept.
People look you in the eyes and say,

Do you recognize me?
You want to, good God, you want to.
They rescued you, bathed you, waited for you.

Come back. Become yourself again. Stay still
while they remove the ventilator, the oxygen,
the feeding tube, the catheter and the PICC line.

If you're lucky, your father holds your hand,
your mother brushes your hair,
your spouse helps you stand again.

The nurse asks, *Have you ever been drunk?*
This is what it will be like.
Lift your chin. Look at the horizon.

Recall what exists beyond these walls: the gorgeously
ordinary river city, the elegant regularity of bus schedules,
kingfishers plunging into the muddy channel.

I. Inhale

If You Hand Me the Right Map

I know the specific line of coast, the surge of shore break, the backroads into town. I know which sidewalk cafes get drenched in warm amber light, which alleys lead back to the office when I've taken too long at lunch. I know the emptied-out apartment after a lover fades into thin air, the unrest when the quad swells with protesting students, placards, police in riot gear. I could tell you of the tired gladness of crossing dusty yellow hills toward home. I could show you where I live, work, sleep. Where I linger over coffee and a newspaper. Where I listen to idle laughter mixing with the effervescent crash of breakers. Where I am bored and elated, heartbroken and satisfied. Where I lay out picnic lunches. Where I slide my finger under an envelope flap and tear. The white seam splitting open. The yawns and sighs. The *mmm hmms* and *ohs* and quietest of *oh no's*.

I want to take you there. But, it's a dreamscape. It's a place I inhabit when I sleep. I dip into and out of the subterranean tunnels of my dreams and the dreams of others. As a teenager, I rode one perfect wave into and out of my father's co-worker's dream, and for the length of one nightmare, my childhood friend and I were one person.

The first time I lucidly walked through an empty apartment, ran my hand across the kitchen table and understood it was my dreaming life, it might have been the first time I grasped the theory of a multiverse. I am here and there and every other somewhere: I am walking down some street or beach or hallway in a kaleidoscope of daughter universes. Time projects holograms, heat mirages, sphinx-like apparitions. For an instant, the world lights up, and I'm stepping into cobalt water, inhaling heavy marine air or unfurling a red and white checkered cloth. A strand of hair blows across my face, a thumb brushes my lips, and then it's over.

Life by Bicycle

At four a.m., our cat lays a starling down in the hallway. The bird's complaint sounds like the snapping of green branches. Its eye contains night sky. To soothe it, I bend my words into a gentling music. I make my voice like cool water on sun-warm stone. My husband reveals his bicycle accidents carefully. *I laid my bike down yesterday. Let's go easy.* For years, we've lived without a car; we speak with new fragility. We've come to accept the gravity of traveling without walls of steel and glass. Our bodies are part sky, part bird. We move through air alone.

The Compass Rose Spins Like a Ouija Board Planchette

for Rina Borodkin Moog

36°07'04.5"N, 86°47'48.8"W

It happens that we might live
a life which isn't ours. Desire rises:

it's mercury, it's honey.
It doesn't matter.

We spend whole lifetimes getting
unlost and unlost and unlost.

For years, we could mistake prayers
for blessings. To make sense of them,

work in a church office, preferably one with
a corrupt minister. Study her boots, her rhetoric.

Serve warm cake. Who knows what nourishes
the wanderer?

32°00'40.9"S, 115°33'03.8"E

You could be a solitary woman
who has gone days without talking,

traveled by taxi, subway, train, airplane, car,
bus, ferry, and foot

to the rocky prominence
of a remote island

to watch for the green flash of rock parrots,
to eat a meal of apples, cheese and tea.

Spray lifts off a cresting wave,
sand brushes limestone.

You could be this woman.
You could be another.

36°09'20.9"N, 86°47'00.4"W

Another possibility:
metal takes air in civil union.

A woman on a bicycle is a theorem
about the adamant body.

It's solemn enough until she starts to coast,
light superimposed on water, flowing

over bedrock. The air thrums with starlings.
Heat—heart-built heat:

a woman, a murmuration,
a cascade of sparks falling

past arc welders on a scaffolding.
She carries herself through air

whispering, *steady, steady*.
The day echoes a recurring dream

until dawn interrupts. The thin line of a heron
flies over the rooftops of the city skyline.

46°11'33.6"N, 114°10'19.8"W

Let us ignore a few things,
but not everything.

A jackrabbit stirs the sagebrush,
a red fox disappears

behind the Hideout bar.
Finches, then river water, glint

beyond the scrim of
song and neon.

The jukebox is playing Willie
and we sip tequila in silence,

waiting for the evening chorus.
No one is sure how we will get home.

36°08'03.6"N, 86°47'40.1"W

Midnight midcontinent, and I'm hip-deep
in ice water.

Two storms, St. Jude. Don't let this be
my lost cause.

My father is on a broken boat circling
off the coast of Baja.

He scowls like Captain Haddock,
rain mixes with saltwater in his beard.

A hurricane with my dead friend's name
scrapes across the Atlantic.

Midnight midcontinent,
I'm hip-deep.

Fury was never hers,
but I'll take it. I'll take it all.

With my right hand, I hold the Pacific at bay.
With my left hand, I invite the storm to come.

47°11'32.7"N, 114°5'16.8"W

My father labors in a barn, casting
a Buddha of cement and sutra.

One bird, then another
dips over the fence wire.

Say's phoebes keep a vigilant choreography:
barn roof nest to water spigot, to fencepost, to roof,

a woven two-bird swoop.
The sun hasn't risen, yet

my father breathes on his hands,
fixes a prayer into stone.

45°38'09.2"N, 113°26'36.2"W

We need to know what we know.
Damp air scours the wild onion
as clouds scrape low.

A buck-and-rail fence line
marks an old homestead
where mint still grows.

A seismic shift sets the geyser clock
to keep new time. Beetle blight
and summer burns throw

new points of balance.
Warblers hide while singing
and the grayling arc

in the river, beyond Wisdom.

35°29'23.9"N, 91°58'21.6"W

Rain sweeps fog off the brackish water
as we drift in an aluminum boat.

The gravity of this world is a constant.
So much can't be that can't be undone.

Yet, today we have alligator gar, armadillos,
and a heron scouting the shoals.

My husband's cast whistles
into white air.

Trail Map of the Sawtooth Mountains

From ridgeline to draw,   shadows flow

      past skreefalls of   stilled tumult.

Tones of elk-scratched   white pine resin   linger on the air.

      Wind shaves the water   like planed wood.

      Time has the vaporous tail of a comet.

Midlife:

      the unlikely dream   of a white-haired mountain goat.

You become wasp-wild.

      It feels like whiplash

      like snow-glare on granite peak.

In the evening,   the elk,   the deer,   and the light

ease into the valley pastures.   Uncontained fire clears

a ruthless path.   Come September   all this will be gone.

Conception

That summer we learned the doe's bark
meant *come*. In dry grass near a barbed wire fence
edging the woods, the fawn's wobbly body
matched how we felt when we finally understood
what we'd done. Some sounds aren't meant

to be made lightly. Our girl appeared when
a snowfall hushed the city. Ice burdened
power lines; block by block the city went dark.
I gathered candles, sliced persimmons,
held a prayer to St. Jude.

My mind was deep in a poem. Moonlit snow
crusted the hollyhock: her father and
I must have made that doe's exhale.
Oh, St. Jude. All the ways we say *come, come*
in a language we don't know.

That August

bats poured out of the attic
and cycloned up in dusk's half-light.

We knew nothing. We believed
we were still young. Night birds spoke
beautiful nonsense.

Shadows soothed as if made
of water. Knowing nothing, we slept,
foot cupped by foot.

The almanac had failed us,
that much we knew. But
we didn't want to know everything,

we couldn't. For a hundred years
the lightning rod on our house
taunted the sky to try its worst.

Everything held together,
each piece of timber in its place.
One needs such facts as a kind of faith.

For decades, I've dreamed of wading
into a river of water hyacinths,
easing into pale pink on blue.

Listen, this is an aubade. At dawn,
the bats returned. How quietly
they tucked back under our eaves.

Fugitive Colors and Other Complications
With the Transitory

For Paula Modersohn-Becker (1876-1907)

If you push through your own Siberia, listening to your labored breathing, to iced firs tinkling. If the crowning flares an aura beyond the annulled boundaries of your body. If your baby girl's legs kick with fierce sureness and weight your hands with wonder. Those first nights, if you sleep in the blurred narcotic dark and find yourself half-awake on a taiga rimmed with stars, then you know too. Perhaps as Galileo knew, sitting in his damp garden charting Europa, Callisto, Io. A parallax calculation reveals the heavens have moved. The phosphorescent swirl of a moonlit tide, a comet's gauzy drape. What isn't a study of heaven? Those hushed mornings matching the palette's bismuth yellow to the yellowhammers quaking the garden light. That unstill dusk in Cezanne's bowl of apples. You said, *What a shame.* Let us ghost awhile together and be unafraid of the body, friable as a dragonfly wing. I don't want us to misunderstand each other, don't want to misspeak. The spectral smear of night's spin latches to its fixed center, a celestial pole. *What a shame:* to miss your girl's toe-to-heel twirl across the studio floor. I would keep this watch as long as I am able, and more.

...

[Our imaginations fail us. During the first post-partum hemorrhage, my husband and I had a conversation about whether our insurance covered trips to the emergency room.]

Lullaby in Blue

Oh, my whip-poor-will, my blue plum, my dandelion clock. You've filled the thistle with lemon yellow finches, made the creeks lilt and warble for another day of quiet song. In the cool sea tonight, otters loll in hammocks of kelp. Little guppy, flying fish, do you know? This is yours. Honeybees hum each other warm in their hives. Luna moths spin down from sweetgum heights. Whales sing off the coast of Tasmania, in the Sea of Cortez. Tonight, tonight the sky is gentle, and the waves whisper *hush* on the shore. Rest now, like a bluehead wrasse in its coral reef. Sea lions bark at the bonfire moon. Oh, little one, you're a sweet oatcake. Here are chestnuts for your pockets and a jar of lightning bugs. Tonight, let me do the worrying, let me shush the ghosts with tea and milk. I'll float the blanket down on you. You nestle here beside me, like a clam tucked in its sandy bed.

...

[The ER doctor said, *I'm sorry, it's the middle of the night, and I'm tired. Stand up. Let's see what happens.*]

Necessary Fictions

Each day repeats its routine.
Dawn backlights roofs and treetops.

You stand at a window, morning opens
like a scene on a stage.

A man in loose slacks and horn-rimmed glasses
walks two statuesque dogs down the street,

the morning paper tucked under his arm.
A girl arabesques as she dismounts a bicycle

on a café patio. A man whistles as he
leans against a lamppost, exhales

a miniature nimbus. Destiny as theater:
everyone acting orderly, following cues.

A pitcher of water is on the table,
each chair is on its mark.

You sigh at the window, one hand on the sill.
As if someone shakes a sheet of copper,

thunder erupts. Tell yourself you will be here
tomorrow.

II. Exhale

...

[My doctor's nurse was annoyed. I called every day and every day she said, *It's normal. You're fine.*]

Jeanne Baret, After Tahiti

Don't tell me what is too much
to ask of this life.

I wanted to see what could be
seen.

Commerçon and I dreamed, fought, and agreed
on one thing: knowledge is worth

the biggest of gambles.
Rules matter little.

And safety?
Safety is illusory.

He relented, and trained me
in how to hold myself

like a man. How to walk,
how to joke, curse, stare.

I starved off the baby weight,
roughed up my hands,

cut my hair, bound my breasts,
and boarded the *Étoile*.

Commerçon met me
as a stranger, the ship's naturalist.

I became his valet.

*

We sailed away

from his dead wife,
our dead son,

my poverty, his wealth.

The sea looked sullen
like rain-shadowed hills.

The sky was shifty:
in turns merciful and cruel

immense with nothingness.

*

We had an audience.
Scrutiny, lust.

Commerçon commanded
that I carry this, do that.

He acted powerful;
I practiced camouflage.

To the crew, I was the odd, thin boy.
I muttered *eunuch*; they retreated.

*

My breasts chafed in the salt and damp,
bled into the bindings.

My only respite:
cool night air drifting in a porthole.

Each dawn, I rebound myself.

*

Commerçon ate with the captain.

In private, we worked side by side.
On deck, I was on my own.

The men wanted to see me piss,
wanted to see how I'd eat a leg of meat.

I performed ugly until I passed.

Late in the dark cabin,
Commerçon would enter with starlight

and hand me some wine, or bread.

*

A storm confused the sea and sky.
Then, we drifted into translucent blue.
It was as if we were sailing above the horizon.

When the Tahitians outed me,
the crew made a collective sound
like a tidal wave sucking out to sea.

I was on my own.

They found me kneeling in the ferns,
collecting noni cuttings.

Some desires burn into fury,
burn everything, burn out.

I crawled back
across the wrack line,
up the gangplank.

They watched me drag myself into the cabin.

*

When the roiling began, I knew
it wasn't seasickness.

I stayed some distance from my body,
labored when it was time.

When we landed, we took everything—
the specimens we had collected,
the notebooks full of charcoal sketches.

I left the crew's child to Mauritius Island

and kept a heliconia blossom, a cassis cornuta shell,
and a blue lorikeet for myself.

It took a long, long time to get home.

Annie Londonderry Sells Advertising Space on Her Shirtwaist

I knew nothing about a bicycle except for the fishmonger who creaked past the tenement building in rusty dawn light, but I became the woman bicycling around the world to win a bet between two rich men. The men and the bet could be more fiction than I. Come Friday, there wasn't enough to pay the milkman. Women passed things back and forth through open windows: a potato, a little flour, a complaint disguised as a prayer. A gentle husband peddled used shoes, anything. I knew every sound the neighbors made: the fights, the lovemaking, the scrape of empty pots becoming emptier. I knew too much about the claustrophobia of a woman without enough. This body contains spectacles. I sold my name first.

Marie Curie Contemplates Gravity While Her Daughters Perform a Trapeze Act

A daughter vaults and whirligigs through space,
emits a spectral light we know but cannot hold.

She claps chalk on her hands,
deftly climbs a rope ladder

up and up. Nothing to do but watch
her defiance: a somersault

above the peach tree, a pirouette midair.
She forgets the scrape

of carriage wheel on gravel,
lifts a curtain of house sparrows,

and lands on a mattress with
a queen's wave. All night,

one daughter follows the other
up into the dark branches of dreams,

jackknifes legs against starlight,
flips revolutions on a crossbar

I can't ever quite see—just a ray of
moonlight sliding sideways through her fists.

Elizabeth Eckford's Walk Toward Central High School
September 4, 1957

Let no old woman spit on a girl.
Let no girl know the snarls
of a mob. Let a girl have more
to shield herself than gingham
and a pair of tortoise shell glasses.
Let a girl in tortoise shell glasses
know the ferocity of a hawksbill
turtle. Let the city bus driver
be heroically prompt.

Let a girl remind us what shouldn't be,
yet sometimes must be, survived alone.
Let a girl know how to turn herself
into a crowbar, a library, a dogwood.
Let a girl be fifteen. Let her be called
Liza, or Lizzie, or Beth. Let a girl be.

Notes For a Future Argument with My Daughter

I want to break a window
with one swiftly thrown china plate.

Because it is impossible to be a good girl.
Because someone has to call the bullies out.

Because I flinch
at the smell of money.

Because my fear for you is
the size of a dying ocean.

Because you need Blue Copper butterflies,
Common Sooty-Wings, Atlantis Fritillarys,

and California Sisters. Goddammit,
you need to know the basic grace of

a California Sister. Because I need you
to know. Because a good girl is like Halley's Comet.

Because someone will keep telling you
to be a good girl. Because there is so much left

unspoken. Because all night long I listen to
the blue dark for the ember glow of

one owl. Because I prefer a practical house
and this is my house. Because a poem is

a kind of necessary solitude. Because
nothing is mine alone—

not these hands, not these words,
not this paper. Because a poem will

redefine the boundaries of us.
Because boundaries disappear.

Leda Confesses to Helen

The sky was absolute and mine
before it was overtaken

with a white tempest.
History shape-shifts the narrative:

I transformed myself in pursuit
of him. All animal, he hunted me.

For centuries, we took turns
pursuing and fleeing, depending on

who was talking, and what
they wanted us to be.

I prefer the versions where
I am wild manifest.

Except for the men, suffering
as if dry land yaws

and sheers beneath them,
the sea is yours.

Do you understand?
What you see blurs,

comes into focus,
blurs.

The sky was mine;
the sea is yours.

Talk to Me: A Wunderkammer
for M.

You've done this before, do you remember? Let two people sit side by side on a Ferris wheel. Let their knees touch. Let them have enough tickets to exhaust the pleasures of the midway: mustard dripping off a corn dog, ping pong balls tossed into bowls of goldfish, darts exploding balloons, wet kisses behind the photo booth curtain.

*

More: even before the words come, a baby learns to sign for it. Let's name it as it is, then—necessary. *I want you. To know. I need. More. More, more, more.*

*

A porcupine caribou traverses a glacial ice field. Let mystery work its way. This way, perhaps.

*

Let's be real. Until 1910, in Hot Springs, Arkansas, African American bathhouse attendants were required to rub mercury on bathers' syphilis chancres. Attendants had to provide their own gloves. After 1910, mercury rubbing was not "required." Don't be naive.

*

In Christie's auction house, a fossilized elephant bird egg the size of a human head goes up on the auction block. Somehow, this is comforting. In a place you can find with a plane ticket and a map there exists an artifact of this desire to go on; its proportions are colossal. You want to hold it in your arms.

*

On the remote island of Nikumaroro, Amelia Earhart's blue leather shoe waited to be found. It was a terrible game of hide and seek. Even the shoe thought so.

*

In your childhood toy box: a green rabbit's foot, a rusty horseshoe, an alarm clock with Betty Boop in a black negligee and garter belt. Her puppy dog bobbed his head side to side. Tick, tock. Are you lucky? That's still up for debate.

*

Kiryat Yam, Israel: dozens of people have reported seeing a mermaid. She likes sunsets. Don't we all?

*

Among the sleeping landmines of the Demilitarized Zone between North and South Korea, endangered red-crowned cranes strut and loft with their heads thrown back in desire. Such a loud ballet, an improbable peace.

*

This is and is not how you do it. Heather, learn to make enough from not enough and not enough. Learn again, damn it.

*

Speyer Cathedral, Germany, year 1146: St. Bernard of Clairvaux prays before a painting of a nursing Madonna and child. He experiences the distinct sensation of breast milk spraying his lips. Do you understand what I am saying? A man feels something brush his lips as he kneels in the chiaroscuro light of dawn. It mystifies. Hundreds of years later, we are still talking about it.

*

At this moment in the Florida Everglades, a ghost orchid trembles as a sphinx moth alights.

*

There. There it is. Don't ask how you know.

...

[Everything is okay until it isn't. Gaps appear between all we know and all we will never know.]

Survival Handbook, Abridged

Anticipate shock. Sleep deprivation makes you
see things that are and are not true. Use your senses.
Stand your ground, then play dead.

Head uphill. Avoid falling objects.
Take care with what is hidden
underwater. Stay low. Swim. Make noise.

Look taller than you are. Project calmness.
Do not make sudden moves. Moderate
the tone, volume, and speed of your speech.

Take shelter, underground if possible. Stay away
from windows. Drink plenty of water. Don't
overexert yourself. Move quickly. Seek higher ground.

Layer clothes. Wear leather: gloves, hat, good boots.
Keep your neck covered. Apply pressure. Use
what is available: punk, thistle down, gunpowder.

Listen for a roaring sound. Travel during the day.
Only drive if necessary. Tell others where you are going.
Seal doors, windows, and fireplaces. If you can't see it,

you can't be sure it's there. Learn to
improvise. Constantly orient yourself.
Plan all of your moves. Expect aftershocks.

An Early Theory of Time and Space

Beneath black poplars, crocus blossoms.
Persephone's blouse sinks into still water.

III. Let the Ventilator Breathe for You

...

[This body, the marble floor: a perplexity of color.]

General Anesthesia

Perhaps it is too easy to forget.
3, 2, 1. The body levitates

above lodestone earth
as the world vaults and spins.

Your hands roam like small catboats
skirring every surface.

A nurse ties you down, the surgeon
demands more sedative.

No wreck, no aftereffect,
only a backscattering of light and a glide.

...

[Galaxies. God. Time warps. We unlearn everything.]

Ways to Disappear

Pull the wardrobe door shut tight and step
into a snowy forest lit with one lamppost.

Follow the rabbit in the waistcoat. Leap after the ever-boy
over the rooftops of London. Sail for a year and a day

away from the simmering dinner pot, mom.
Grip the bedpost and ride a vortex

above the cornfields. Outsmart
One-Eyed Willy's booby traps by tunneling

under a wishing well. Climb into
a lightning-charged DeLorean. Punch through

a ceiling tile and scale the elevator shaft.
Push the fireplace corbel just so

to open the door hidden in the bookshelf.
Take your great need to the seventh floor corridor;

the Room of Requirement will appear. Crawl through
the secret passage into Jupiter Jones' junkyard hideout.

Run along the train roof and
grab the helicopter's landing skids.

Pull on a leather skullcap and aviator glasses
then slip into Bermuda blue.

Tonight, At the Santee Drive-in Movie Theatre

Here we are, rolling down the windows of a Volkswagen squareback to a set of car speakers. A hazy, late-July sunset casts a thin silhouette of my parents. My best friend is here, always here. Everyone sits where they can: on aluminum lawn chairs and ice chests, in the open trunk, on the roof. We pass around a bucket of popcorn and listen to the hush as floodlights cut and speakers squawk to life. We must be wearing stripes: brown, teal, burnt orange. We watch *Rocky, Grease, Footloose*. Here, again: we choose our spot under the bird-laced electric blue, hitch our Keds on the Chevy tailgate, drink Dr. Pepper through licorice straws. We watch *Edward Scissorhands, Reality Bites*. We'd watch anything. And here: in Chuck Taylors and flannel shirts, at the edge of asphalt and alfalfa, tossing sleeping bags into the bed of the truck. The pillows keep the dizzying scent of a teenage boy with thick, wavy tresses that twine my fingertips. We forget to watch the double feature. My best friend eats a hot pretzel with mustard. And then she's gone and I'm reversing into place, unhooking the hatchback and unzipping a sleeping bag to a man who unwinds everything I know. We watch *The Matrix, Mulholland Drive*. Uncertain of the narrative we half-sleep, half-dream beneath shaggy-headed palm trees and meteor showers. Then, we're here, handing crumpled dollars to the guy wearing a retro *Goonies* t-shirt. My sister-in-law and I take our place side by side on fold-out beach chairs in uncanny flamingo pink light. We've snuck out, barely remembering how it's done. At home: pajamas, teeth brushing, story time with grandma. Here: *Atomic Blonde*, the crackle of radio air, low murmurs, tires rolling past. A hush ripples across the still hot blacktop, and then it begins.

Dreamboats

Han Solo shells peanuts
and sips beer at the bar.
Reclining on peat moss,
MacGyver cradles his head
with one hand as he whispers:
Ursa Major. He slides his
other hand up: *Polaris.*
This luscious misrule of men.
Still. Decades of forever and *still*
Lloyd Dobbler glumly drums
a steering wheel. Bo Brady
dismounts his motorcycle,
scuffs up the boat dock
in false moonlight. Waiting,
always waiting, this faithful
brood. Jake Ryan leans back, hands
in his pockets. Face smokes a cigar,
plans the next noble con.
This yearning, a synaptic
constellation of pop stars.
Maverick leans into the curves
of Highway 1, aviator glasses
glinting in dusk's sharp light.
I'm still there too, a blonde
in Wayfarers and cutoff shorts,
flipping the cassette tape
to hear, again, *Boys of Summer,*
one arm an ode, exalting
in the car window's frame of sun.
Ren McCormack and Johnny Castle
don't hesitate; they're ready
for the next song. Ah, yes and there:

our ranch house lit up
like a mercury vapor streetlight.
My father in a bathrobe
waiting, while I make it
home by curfew.

At Daybreak

We'd gather on the cliff and lean our elbows
against the fence. Everything felt close.
The murmur of voices, breakers, gulls drifted

in the air, just beyond the sandstone edge.
Light poured down the hills and defined
waves folding beyond the shoreline.

Surfers appeared—black shadows in a white fog.
They glistened like sleek, muscular sea lions.
As the sun burned away the marine layer

they rolled to the surface and disappeared
into the dark water. All day long,
my friend and I watched those leonine boys.

We knew their bodies without touching them;
their uniform was a pair of shorts, nothing more.
Boys with salty eyelashes, sun-browned

hands, feet. They formed our understanding
of Greek mythology. Their skin emanated
radiant heat after sundown. Ours did too.

Vigil

Midnight tucks around a house lit with one lamp.
A man sits at a kitchen table. He's our man, and he is alone
and not alone and so alone.

There should be a note for him to find, long forgotten
in an old coat pocket. There should be a silent figure
crossing the room to put a hand on his cheek.

Glass utters against wood. Morning composes itself
of chimney smoke and dew. It will take a lifetime
to see him clearly. It may never be enough.

If You and I Said *Fuck it*, and Bought the Ranch in Montana

I'd have hands that could set bone
or arc a two-bit axe.

I'd study how gravity pulls sugar through apple,
what it means to straighten a river,

to keep a clutch of cedar waxwings
coming back.

You'd have a mountain ridge rain shadow,
a distortion in your voice like trout under creek water.

Your hands would untangle fishing nets,
or our child's wet hair. You'd listen to how stillness

breaks in front of an avalanche,
the way elk disappear into serviceberry,

what silences surround an instarring gypsy moth.

Yesterday's Bestiary for Tomorrow

The ivory-billed woodpecker knockers the swampy bottomlands with an axiom on survival. We memorize its red mohawk and high-pitched toot *kent, kent, kent,* then search the bald cypress and tupelo as if looking for Aristotle's half-soul. If desire can be prayer we might say, *Let us be here together.* How we listen, these little epochs.

*

A school of akule columns into the hosanna of us, a trembling knot of this every only now. A shirring big-eyed wonder-mess of unified gold shine. Boundaries redefined mid-whirl. Now a globe, an atoll, a flying buttress. Togetherness manifest, togetherness solidified, togetherness as an act of defiance. As trust of other.

*

When it comes, it is the sensation of peering through a View-Master: sage scrub hills of San Clemente Island invaded by sea. Kodachrome tints circa 1979: aqua and goldenrod. I scissor-kicked beyond the 3-D loom of the cliffs, listening to the water sigh against sandstone. My brother, face down beside me, rasped through a snorkel. He popped up blinking, coughing. A manta ray bigger than us: a diamond of night sky fluttering below. Our feet touched nothing. We weren't afraid.

This Body Fixed in Place

Woman as granite   as poppy hillside   sharp as grassfire

quantum shimmer   blurred edges

an indigo study   of blue   of violet   of blue

woman as fog on water   as nebula   as chalcedony

willow bark tincture   hazel catkin

for you   I take vows   in the abbey   of restraint

I stay   staying   still

an oak   on   oak savanna   I walk towards

open   I open   I keep   opening   keep   keeping

The Northern Pacific Gyre

A universe of bad dreams
spins its heavy tail.

My Fretting Ghosts Keep Watch

They breathe in the far corner of the hospital room.
Elbow to elbow, they try to stay out of the way.

Defying visiting hours, they sigh, rustle, wait.
After the surgeon gives his post-op report and leaves

my grandfather hands me his handkerchief.
I can almost hear him say, *sweetie, sweetie.*

My mother-in-law holds the silence
surrounding the terrible truth about

the limits of our bodies. Doors exhale.
Machines beep and tick with vigilance.

The footsteps of the invisible
nurses shuffle past without pause.

All We Don't Know: When Waking Up

My mother looks god-awful. The night nurses have shaky hands. My father tears six pages off a wall calendar and points. *It's Thursday now.* My husband said his goodbyes a week ago. I can't remember our telephone number. When I close my eyes, I see neon. I'm told the baby is stoic. I have pneumonia, radioactive breast milk. This might be a heart attack, might be brain damage. My hands are unrecognizable. Someone washed my hair, painted my toenails. The respiratory therapist yells, *Try harder.* When he returns at two a.m., he kneels and draws blood so, so gently I name him the Zen master of needles. I've been dreaming about juggling too many things, dreaming I've been stuck in a dark airport terminal. Nighttime quiet of the ICU: the loneliest thing I know.

In the Unlikeliest of Places, Joy

The transporter sings
while pushing my gurney

down a corridor. The gospel of
his voice surrounds us

like an invisible cathedral.
For the length of one hymn,

I am Bede's sparrow
gliding down ember-lit halls.

In the distance, rain blows
through an open window.

The Smiths Address the Quandary of Love & Illness

My surgeon had a delightful lope to his gait. *I know. It sucks,* he said. I trusted him then, knew he read me right at a glance. I handed my mother a bag with my clothes. She slipped my wallet and car keys into her purse. The procedure was supposed to be brief, routine—time for her to get a latte. She was probably bored.

It wasn't routine. Eight days later, as I take my first difficult hospital shower, one hand running through my hair, one hand bracing against the wall, I shakily sing the Smiths: *Girlfriend in a coma, I know, I know, it's serious.* The song loops as I unpuzzle myself. I recall the soap opera I used to watch while sprawled on the living room floor those lazy childhood afternoons with my mother ironing nearby. A secret love affair or blackmail plot unraveled around some beautiful person sleeping in a hospital bed. Over time, the beautiful person changed, the plot changed, but everything else seemed to stay the same. It is all I know of comas.

In day-to-day life, I like a well-made bed: smooth sheets, cool pillow. I like a fridge stocked with milk and cheese, bread and coffee. I prefer the sharpest cheddar, the darkest espresso, and sourdough. I don't do drama, don't waiver.

Morrissey croons, *There were times when I could have murdered her.* Me too. A lifetime of actions slingshot through the present moment. All my clumsy, bullheaded ways. Each infrared heat trace in someone's angry look. A short list: I hold on too long, I get indignant, judge-y. Yes, sure, I'm a real bitch now and then. When I was nineteen, my best friend and I were on a road trip with some guy we knew. He wouldn't get in the car unless he could drive. I was driving. *Get in,* I said. He didn't budge. *Come on, just get in already.* Sour from last night's beer, he said, *No.* So, I drove off and left him in an empty parking lot with nothing but a closed-up storefront, an unmarked stretch of highway, and flat, gray, winter fields. It was a long while before there was an off-ramp we could use to turn around. When we went back for him, he was in a phone booth making a collect call to his mother.

In this now-and-never-after, I don't want to tattoo regret somewhere private—on this crest of hipbone or handsbreadth of thigh—I don't want to leave it for a lover to undress in the impossible future.

How will I know when I've lost too much blood? I had asked my OBGYN. *You will pass out,* she said. She did not say what we both knew. By then, it would be too late.

I had driven my mother and I to the hospital and waited on a startlingly white couch in the intake room. I had negotiated payment plans with the customer service rep while praying I wouldn't blackout in that public place. The rep wanted payment upfront, in full. I had measured my language, discussed coverage plans and deductibles. Some nightmares are a shock of color, and nothing else.

I taught rhetoric: my job was careful, measured language. Would a little hysteria have served me better? Hysteria: let's not follow that word too far. I didn't have the right words. I overthought the wrong words. Worse, the surgeon hadn't read my chart, hadn't traced the record backward to see the clues. No one understood. Not me, not him, not the boyfriend in the song. It was serious.

My, my, my, my, my, my baby, goodbye. That downbeat: it's so cheerful. Catchy. Morrissey vamps a little in the pout, the jutting jawline. It could be 1987. A spray of water slides down my closed eyes, my shoulder blades.

Whenever this is, I am listening for the first time.

Scintigraphy

Breathe deep and inhale the radioactive mist,
then lie still while radionuclides are injected
into your vein. Wait. To stay calm, recall
your favorite surf break. Old Man's:

the big, slow fold of ocean
you used to surf with your father.
He's waiting for you now
outside the nuclear medicine room,

just as he watched outside the break line
to see what might come—a ride, or
a crash, each spectacular in different ways.
The reef verged on a nuclear power plant.

You'd turn your back to the horizon,
look at the facility's vaulted roofline, and
accept what you soaked in as a tradeoff for
the way it felt to glide across the rise of water.

Now, you obey the nurse and turn, arms raised,
hands behind your head as if good behavior will
improve the results. Rotating images of your lungs
appear: the branches of arteries glow,

a tree radiant with snow. The doctor says
your lungs are the most normal he's ever seen.
You're free to go. The day is almost gone.
Low rays of light blur autumn redbud and ash.

IV. Breathe Again

All We Don't Know: Of Budgeting

We need what we need. A birth, a hemorrhage, a hysterectomy, multiple blood transfusions, six days on life support. An ER doctor, three obstetricians, a hematologist, pulmonologist, cardiologist, infectious disease specialist, nuclear medicine specialist, anesthesiologist, priest. Teams of nurses, respiratory therapists, a speech pathologist, physical therapist, lactation specialist, family counselor. An ultrasound, cystoscopy, ten chest x-rays, pulmonary V/Q scan, pathology report. Blood products, morphine, radioactive technetium macro aggregated albumin, technetium DTPA. Feeding tube nutritional supplements, metoclopramide, antibiotics, Diflucan, Tylenol, iron. Sum total: $131,004.62.

Evidence for the Flawed World

We forget our luck—good God, do we forget.
We wake and the world solidifies: mussed sheets,
a bedside table, a glass of water gleaming like mercury.

Like the woman who fled with Buddha's left canine
hidden in the knot of her hair, we salvage ephemera
against loss: Van Morrison's *Brown Eyed Girl* on vinyl,

our child's baby teeth, the Führer Globe, a narwhal tusk.
Nothing makes sense, but we love, or fear, or know
an awe that recollects us to what matters—

every damn crazy thing. We wake beneath
snow-hushed birch or in some strange bed
wise to our luck. And we forget.

Near-Death Experience: a Counter-Narrative

I wish there had been angels. Some stupid *no shit* proof. Idiot-proof proof: the tunnel, the light, the unshakeable knowing. It is not uncommon now to have a friend ask, *Did you see God?* while we eat appetizers or idly watch a bartender roll a Bloody Mary, as if I took a vacation to heaven and might have glimpsed him sunbathing on the beach outside his villa. God in swim trunks, spritzing Hawaiian Tropic on his shoulders—a Hugh Jackman look-alike diving into whitewater.

Instead, interstellar cold and grainy radio static. An endless waiting. It was like I spent a week in an airport terminal with the electricity out. Jostled by unseen bodies. Waiting, just waiting in Dante's land of sighs. My mind was empty.

I didn't know what I was missing, didn't remember the peach I ate that June day with my head hanging out of the car window and my windblown hair sticking to the juice trickling down my arms. I didn't remember my unstoppable cry just three weeks prior as I held my daughter for the first time, both of us safe and whole. That cry lasted for hours: every cell knowing the grace of her skin against mine. The nurse wheeled us out of the delivery room and I cried in the elevator, through the winding corridors all the way to the nursery. Dawn came and I was still crying when I sang the first lullaby. Such clean joy, those tears.

But in that empty galaxy, I forgot all of it. I sighed my sighs. Then, through the darkness, a man's voice. *Do you want to hear a poem?* Yes. As I listened, I recognized the lines. The poem was mine. One poem and I remembered myself again, all I loved—the sugar pines, the figs, the men. I forgot the forgetting and surfaced.

Days later, I learned that during each shift my husband took by my hospital bed, he read to me from the book I'd left on my nightstand. My father, wild-haired and unshaven, took a dog-eared collection of my poems, and read from those.

Magritte's *Golconda* as Treatise on Post-Traumatic Stress Disorder I

Another kingdom in ruin that doesn't know it yet.
No rustle of coattails. No echo of footsteps.

No murmurs, no car horns, no breeze—
only the sweet scent of Brylcreem and a deluge of men

on the city skyline: a dark fog of suits
bowler hat after bowler hat, levitating

as if rain stopped midair. They tuck pocket watches
into waistcoats, shift valises from one hand to the other,

begin to tap their Wingtips on thin air.
Everyone has somewhere to be.

Below, people bump into walls.
In a fit of confusion, men forget how to read

the sky, how to read their lover's face.
They slosh dirty vermouth, smoke cigars,

stumble into dark apartments, and sleep
beside strange wives.

At sun-up, barbers sharpen razors on leather strops,
frown at the knotted weir of sky above them.

All We Don't Know: Of Hysterectomies

If the orchestra hall is demolished. If the subtle twinges of a violin sonata and the after-hum are lost. If the tiny filaments of stereovilli stopped fluttering in the labyrinthine inner ear. If we don't think of it as mythical. Instead, nuanced. A ripple-effect of muscle and nerve. If we don't dismiss a woman as neurotic. Frigid. Disinterested. If phantom pain exists, real as sutures, as scar tissue. If we say amputation.

Terra Incognita

I have never seen all of my father's tattoos. Out of my peripheral vision, I catch an unfamiliar glimpse of a maple leaf or scythe-glint of blue kimono that disappears under a cuff. I see a metaphor I can't quite decipher, and then it's gone and we are talking about the benefits of all-wheel drive vehicles.

The winter my mother was diagnosed with cancer, my father's body flash burned, a chaparral wildfire. She listened to the prognosis and booked a pre-op appointment. He swallowed a Vicodin, unbuttoned his plaid shirt, and settled into the leather chair for Bill, his tattoo artist. Dad and Bill talked through as much pain as my father could tolerate—kids, grandkids, micro-brewing, surf breaks. After my father's needle-punched torso (followed by shoulders, arms, and flank) were covered with a piece of gauze, my father must have shrugged carefully back into his shirt, shook Bill's hand, and walked into the glare of neon and streetlight. Day after day, session after session. The months wore on.

My mother's swollen and stapled post-op abdomen shrank and healed into a jagged scar. My father's body smoldered into a dragon, a coi, a rising phoenix, a tsunami, a geisha. What images am I missing? I have no idea.

My father has always withdrawn into house chores and helped anyone who needs it, whether they want help or not. I can still hear the whisk of the broom on blacktop as he swept the driveway each Saturday morning. He is Johnny to his mother's sisters and their kids, John Humble to his buddies, and John, plain John to everyone else.

When they were teenagers on their first date, my mother cut her foot on a piece of glass at the beach. My father stripped off his shirt, wrapped up her bleeding foot, and carried her back to the car. And in the fifty years since? Once a month, my mother places a chair for him on the porch, drapes a towel over his shoulders, and cuts his hair.

Each of us has to learn for ourselves about those icy plunges into the open sea at the edge of the world—those unknown places where human love takes us. *Here be dragons,* the earliest mapmakers used to warn. There is so much I can't know. But, I can tell you this: my father's tiny elderly aunt still pats his grizzled cheek and exclaims, *Johnny!* when she leans in for a kiss. And, when I ask my father his tattoo artist's name to make sure I've remembered it right, he says, *Do you want me to book you an appointment? I could ask him a favor. He'd fit you in.*

Naming the Poetry

Some years, it is more difficult
to hear the poems. Music suffers
static. A girl in red boots waits
on the street corner and looks so sad.

Her eyes, smudged with soot,
don't change when her mother hands her
a paper sack full of figs. All of autumn's
oranges refract at lazy angles. I catalog the colors

as if doing an exercise: here are tones
like spessartine garnets, like Ceylon tea.
George calls and describes October's first snow
catching on the haunches of deer

as they nip the last tomatoes from his garden.
On the cabin porch, my father points to falling
needles combed out of the sugar pines by a warm wind.
The lawn turns honey red. *This is a poem, isn't it,* he asks.

My brother tells a story of his day
until I unknot into laughter.
My husband translates old Icelandic poems
while pumpkin roasts.

Here's the shift: it is like a boat listing.
When my hearing weakens, I go to the men I love and
find them pointing here, pointing there, whispering,
Look at that. Look at that.

Magritte's *Golconda* as Treatise on Post-Traumatic Stress Disorder II

In this dream   a barrage of men   leaden the sky

as if dropped   from a squadron   of kitty hawks

a horizon of   trench coats   spit-shined   valises

in this dream   rain-slick men

in gray flannel suits   disappear behind   a smoke screen

of cigar fog   drowned out   by the clamor   of stenographers

in this dream   the dream   disappears

the dream   detonates   the dream loops

the dream sleeps   underground

Don't Let Me Let You Down

The knocking started soon after we moved into the house on the corner of Broadway and nowhere. A stranger helped us carry our sofa up the front steps. I put our mismatched plates in the cupboard. No one tells you how many swaybacked pregnant women will step onto your porch, asking. The sandwiches a neighborhood requires. The glasses of water and calls for an ambulance. I learned to make sack lunches as my belly grew. With the baby on my hip I packed milk and diapers, bus money, directions to the shelter. Later my daughter would try to read my face as I wrapped a sandwich in wax paper, grabbed an apple, some cheese. A woman and I stood in that sieve of dusk. She waited until I met her flint glance across the distance of the tablecloth. *I love you*, she said. Every time I got it wrong. *Take care. Good luck. Bless you*, I would say. How slight we were. Each of us, a hand's breadth of yielding ilium and floating scapula.

Topographical Map of January

When a man telemarks into high country,
his wife, gathering wood in the valley, senses
all the steep inclines between floor and ridge.

She blisters her hands wringing
greywater out of wash. Family makes
a body without boundary.

Worry makes a body somnolent.
To feel the extremities, sometimes
one must lose sensation,

then coax it back, coax it back.
Dry pines creak. The man pushes
hard and harder still, until he glides.

The woman breathes into her hands;
her blood swirls like snow. She draws inward,
lighting embers with her breath.

They heat and hold what space they can.
The valley funnels wind against walls
that solace and confine all at once.

Preparedness Training for Toddlers: Go Find the Neighbor

We look for him
out the kitchen window.

He lights a cigarette, waters the marigolds
as the kettle prattles on our stove.

(At midnight that ever-winter,
I listened to the magnolia shatter.)

She arranges the domestic life of her mouse house;
he takes out his trash. We tap on the glass,

send down kisses with a flourish of hands.
He never fails to look up.

(That winter, ice piled on the roof,
wind snipped the pines.)

She wants to show him her painting.
I say, *Go find Scott*. She sets off running.

We trade crocks of slow-cooked stew;
she chases his dog across the lawn.

(No drag races, no patrol cars, no sirens. Yet,
the imagination runs scenarios; the body responds.)

A storm cloud dusk blurs the skyline. We watch
the porch lights on our street turn on one by one.

After Bikini Atoll

The navy seamen splashed in the aquamarine shallows, subdued the heat with ice cream and beer. Men sat elbow to elbow in government-issued goggles to watch the horizon like a 3-D movie. Everyone cheered at the double sunset, the spectacle of cloud and ash.

Let me stop right here to note the porous twins of atoll and bone. To think of Castle Bravo, of fission yields. To know the implications for Jack, my Jack. As enlisted, as serviceman, as witness. His femur in the service of. His marrow as witness of.

I can't ask my grandfather what he did, how it broke him, how he coped in the long afterwards. What I can tell you: years later, after working the night shift, Jack drove his son to Doheny Beach, curled up in the backseat of his 1957 Chevy Bel Air, and slept his Saturdays away.

Let me go to this edge of shoreline, this arc of time. To locate the lost. To brush the sand off my feet and lay down in the cool shade of the Bel Air. To cradle my head on my arm—that fragile cross of radius and ulna, and share this fractured sleep with him.

Urban Self-Portrait

San Diego. Each palm tree planted in its place. Pelicans skim breakers beyond a wrack line of kelp and sand toys. Coastal sagebrush and California buckwheat shiver on the cliffs. People glint with salt-grit and coconut oil, and talk at a hazy half-pace. This is where you school yourself in lounge chair semantics, cash out your inheritance of sun-blonde nude. On a dock, a burly young man slings yellowtail onto ice. A Steller sea lion appears, disappears, reappears. Do you hear yourself? Are you listening? Stow away such things for tomorrow.

*

Seattle. Light sifts down through fog laden tulip fields as the air trembles with ferry horns on the half hour. Everything blurs in the rain; even your body disappears into mist, into night sky. You want to calculate desire and find it each night outside the window of your studio above the town's one tavern. Men shout *Mama!* and stumble out after last call as the barkeep puts a quarter in the jukebox. The deepest part of night is his—the sharp clink of glass and ice getting tossed into the bus tub, Toby Keith crooning, *I should've been a cowboy, I should've learned to rope and ride.* Unseen above the empty town square, you keep company with the man wiping a dishcloth across the scarred wood of an old bar top. Do you recognize this scene? It's you, it's you.

*

Berkeley. Fog thins coastal live oaks, sun falls
scattershot in blue gum eucalyptus. A street fight
punctures neighborhood calm: teen boys ride the
hard edges of their new voices. At a flower stand,
a girl in fingerless gloves wraps marigolds in brown
paper and twine; a busboy leans on a steamed up
café windowsill. Sliding between sighing
letterpress machines and men in moth-eaten wool,
you find a way to exchange existential doubt for a
plate of curry. Egrets peer into the brackish water
of Strawberry Creek. An elderly man, chicken
bone thin, trembles in the open.

*

Nashville. Learn to love the nights marked by a
musty scent that is the precise dank of
Disneyland's Pirates of the Caribbean bayou, the
sphinx moths in the honeysuckle, the steeples that
pierce *hallelujah* skies. If you can, love the
MoonPies, the evenings tuning a guitar among the
okra flowers, and the lazy domestic creeks.
Summon love as if it will be obedient, just this
once. Call it like you call the cat at the back door
each night at bedtime.

*

Little Rock. At sun-up, a woman runs down the
middle of the street. Be afraid with her as she
looks over her shoulder, yells, blurs into the
distance even as cardinals blush the lace bark elm
above an old man troweling a patch of greens.
Curse the rioting tornadoes, the bullets riddling

abandoned cars into starlight. But, know it's useless: chaos makes house calls in an ill-fitting suit. You might begin speaking in tongues, or you might begin here.

*

Let yourself claim all of this now, and now, and now.

Our First Worst Lesson

Let's think in truths, near as we can get to it.
Object impermanence: a stuffed lion

with a jagged orange sun for a mane
vanishes into a sea of evening air.

A small porcelain bowl
unforms against the floor.

You've gone and done exactly what you feared
you'd do. You disappeared.

How many stories will you not know
how to tell? You battled in the darkness that is

forgetting. Wind slapped windows, tore maples.
You didn't exist, and then you did.

By the grace of *somehow*
by the fact of *so it is.*

It happens.
It will happen again.

You might leave a photograph
of a crescent moon smile,

a dress with tiers of pleated lace
folded in a box in the back of a closet.

Here are your arms, your hands.
Better make them as gentle as you can.

To Begin—

Praise this body, the bones & hematopoietic marrow,
the timekeeper heart & the unfailing lungs.

Praise how it stands & fights & stands again,
a featherweight against the ropes.

Praise the harbor it carves out of
the unlikely ribcage, hipbones, knees.

Praise its brazen loving, for all it has made,
& praise its limits, for which it will exhaust itself

trying to overcome each one at once. Praise
the fidelity of each duct, each letdown reflex,

each substantiation. Praise each muscle,
each act of tenderness. Even the last.

Notes

The epigraph for the collection is from the song "Night Has Turned to Day" by the Fantastic Negrito. *Fantastic Negrito*, © 2016 Blackball Universe. All rights reserved.

"Annie Londonderry Sells Advertising Space on her Shirtwaist." During 1894-1895, Annie "Londonderry" Cohen Kopchovsky rode her bicycle around the world. Legend has it, she set off with a pearl-handled revolver, a change of underwear, and nothing else. I am indebted to the research of Peter Zheutlin in *Around the World on Two Wheels: One Woman, One Bicycle, One Incredible Journey*, 2007.

"Fugitive Colors and Other Problems with the Transitory" responds to Rainer Maria Rilke's poem, "Requiem for a Friend" and Adrienne Rich's poem, "Paula Becker to Clara Westhoff." Paula Modersohn-Becker (1876-1907) was an impressionist painter who died from a postpartum pulmonary embolism eighteen days after giving birth to a daughter named Mathilde.

"Magritte's *Golconda* as Treatise on Post-traumatic Stress Disorder I and II" are based on René Magritte's painting, *Golconda*, 1953. At first I thought this painting was a critique of capitalism and middle-class pressure. But the more that I studied the painting the more I saw it as a study of shell shock—like Sloan Wilson's book about a shell-shocked veteran who has returned to civilian life, *The Man in the Gray Flannel Suit* (1955). The book was made into a movie starring Gregory Peck in 1956.

"Jeanne Baret, After Tahiti." Between 1766-1769, Jeanne Baret sailed around the world on the ship the *Étoile*, and she became the first woman to circumnavigate the world. I first learned about Jeanne Baret while visiting the Western Australia Maritime Museum in Fremantle in

August 2009. I am also indebted to the research of Glynis Ridley in *The Discovery of Jeanne Baret*, 2012.

"Survival Handbook, Abridged" is a found poem made by compressing a 300-page government-issued military survival guide.

"The Smiths Address the Quandary of Love & Illness" includes lyrics from "Girlfriend in a Coma" by the Smiths. *Strangeways, Here We Come,* © 2014 Rhino UK a division of Warner Music UK Ltd. All rights reserved.

"Yesterday's Bestiary for Tomorrow" responds to a series of photographs of akule by Wayne Levin (2013).

Thank You

A few writers left an indelible imprint on this collection, and I am profoundly grateful for my time working by their side. Many, many thanks are due to Theodore Deppe, Martín Espada, Debra Marquart, and Jeanne Marie Beaumont. I am also lucky to have the support of my colleagues and students at the University of Arkansas at Little Rock, my family, and most especially Jeremy and Lila, who gifted me time to write. Stephanie Lenox and Mary Ellen Kubit both deserve trophies for their unfailing encouragement. And finally, I am so damn glad Erin Elizabeth Smith and Jeremy Michael Reed believed in this book. Thank you.

About the Author

H.K. Hummel is the author of two poetry chapbooks, *Boytreebird* (Finishing Line Press, 2013) and *Handmade Boats* (Whale Sound, 2010), and co-author of the textbook *Short-Form Creative Writing: A Writer's Guide and Anthology* (Bloomsbury, 2018). She teaches creative writing at the University of Arkansas at Little Rock, and is one of the founding editors of *Blood Orange Review*.

Other Sundress Titles

Bury Me in Thunder
moira j.
$16

Dead Man's Float
Ruth Foley
$16

Gender Flytrap
Zoë Estelle Hitzel
$16

Blood Stripes
Aaron Graham
$16

Boom Box
Amorak Huey
$16

Arabilis
Leah Silvieus
$16

Afakasi | Half-Caste
Hali F. Sofala-Jones
$16

Marvels
MR Sheffield
$20

Match Cut
Letitia Trent
$16

Passing Through Humansville
Karen Craigo
$16

Divining Bones
Charlie Bondus
$16

Phantom Tongue
Steven Sanchez
$15

Citizens of the Mausoleum
Rodney Gomez
$15

The Minor Territories
Danielle Sellers
$15

Either Way, You're Done
Stephanie McCarley Dugger
$15

Actual Miles
Jim Warner
$15

CPSIA information can be obtained
at www.ICGtesting.com
Printed in the USA
LVHW092047160220
647141LV00002B/12